C000264325

A Young Vic / Wiener Festwochen/Ruhrfestspiele Recklinghausen co-production.
Co-commissioned by Warwick Arts Centre.

Sweet Nothings
by Arthur Schnitzler

in a new version by David Harrower

Sweet Nothings premiered at the Young Vic on 4 March 2010 and then toured to:
Theatre Royal Northampton, Rose Theatre Kingston, Warwick Arts Centre,
Wiener Festwochen, Vestlandhalle Ruhrfestspiele Recklinghausen and
the Teatros del Canal Madrid.

Sweet Nothings
by Arthur Schnitzler
in a new version by David Harrower

Christine **Kate Burdette**
Katharina **Hayley Carmichael**
Mizi **Natalie Dormer**
Fritz **Tom Hughes**
Theodore **Jack Laskey**
Weiring **David Sibley**
Gentleman **Andrew Wincott**

Direction **Luc Bondy**
Set and Light **Karl-Ernst Herrmann**
Costumes **Moidele Bickel**
Sound **Gareth Fry**
Dramaturg **Geoffrey Layton**
Associate Costume Designer **Eva Dessecker**
Assistant Design **Barbara Pral**
Hair and Makeup **Campbell Young**
Costume Supervisor **Fizz Jones**
Casting **Sam Jones**

Stage Manager **Joni Carter**
Deputy Stage Manager **Jenny Grand**
Assistant Stage Manager **Ian Andlaw**
Stage Crew **Ben Porter**
Wardrobe Assistant & Dresser **Freya Groves**
Costumes made by
   Fran Alderson, Mark Costello, Keith Watson
Set built by **Weld-Fab Stage Engineering; Factory Settings**
   and in the Young Vic Workshops by **Emma Hayward,
   Fiona Ryan, Ed Wirtz and Duncan Crockford.**
Carpet **Loophouse**
Cloths **Ken Creasey Ltd**
Scenic Artists **Belinda Clisham, James Cotterill**
Prop Maker **Russell Beck**

Arthur Schnitzler

Arthur Schnitzler was born in Vienna in 1862. His father was a prominent laryngologist treating many of Vienna's most popular performers, so Arthur was surrounded by actors from an early age. Following in his father's footsteps, he studied medicine at the University of Vienna and received his doctorate in 1885. Throughout the following years medicine and writing competed for his time, with writing ultimately taking precedence.

He wrote 32 plays. The most celebrated are *Reigen* (*La Ronde*), *Liebelei* (*Sweet Nothings*) – both filmed by Max Ophüls – *Das weite Land* (*Undiscovered Country*), *Professor Benhardi* and *Anatol*.

In addition, Schnitzler wrote many short novels and stories regarded as the equal of Chekhov's, including *Traumnovelle* (*Dream Story*, adapted as *Eyes Wide Shut* by Stanley Kubrick and Frederic Raphael), *Spiel im Morgengrauen* (*Night Games*) and *Fräulein Else*, in which he invented a first-person stream of consciousness.

He died in his beloved Vienna in October 1931.

David Harrower

David Harrower is an internationally acclaimed playwright. Previous works include: *Knives in Hens*, Traverse Theatre and Bush Theatre, London; *54% Acrylic*, BBC Radio 4; *Kill the Old Torture Their Young*, Traverse Theatre; *The Chrysalids*, NT Connections; *Presence*, Royal Court Theatre and *Dark Earth*, Traverse Theatre; *Blackbird*, Edinburgh International Festival, West End, Manhattan Theatre Club and Sydney Theatre Company; *365*, National Theatre of Scotland. Adaptations include: *Six Characters in Search of an Author*, Young Vic; *Woyzeck*, Edinburgh Lyceum Theatre; *Ivanov*, National Theatre; *The Girl on the Sofa*, Edinburgh International Festival and the Schaubühne Berlin; *Tales from the Vienna Woods*, National Theatre; *Mary Stuart*, the National Theatre of Scotland and *The Good Soul of Szechuan*, Young Vic.

Kate Burdette Christine

Theatre includes: *Gilbert is Dead* (Shining Man), *The Tempest* (Stageworks); *A Midsummer Night's Dream* (British Touring Theatre); *Charley's Aunt* (British Touring Theatre); *Private Lives* (Margate Theatre Royal); *Eyes Catch Fire* (Finborough Theatre); *Where there's a will* (Theatre Royal Bath).

Film and TV includes: *The Dark Side of the Earth* (Jigawatt Films); *The Duchess* (BBC Films); *Capturing Mary* (BBC Television).

Hayley Carmichael Katharina

Theatre includes: *The Fahrenheit Twins* (Told by an Idiot); *Fragments* (C.I.C.T/Théâtre des Bouffes du Nord); *Bliss* (Royal Court); *Casanova* (Told by an Idiot/West Yorkshire Playhouse); *The Maids* (Brighton Festival); *Zumanity* (Cirque du Soleil); *Theatre of Blood* (Improbable/NT); *I'm a Fool to Want You* (Told by an Idiot/BAC); *Streets of Crocodiles* (Complicite/NT); *The Birds* (NT); *Mother Courage* (Shared Experience).

Film and TV includes: *Viva Blackpool* (Channel 4); *Tunnel of Love* (BBC); *One Day* (Stock-pot Productions); *The Emperor's New Clothes* (Redwave Films).

Natalie Dormer Mizi

Film includes: *Casanova* (Touchstone Pictures); *City of Life* (AFM Films); *Flawless* (Magnolia Pictures); *Fencewalker* (Chris Carter).

TV and Radio includes: *The Tudors* (Showtime/BBC); *Miss Marple: Why Didn't They Ask Evans* (ITV); *Rebus* (ITV); *Masterwork* (Fox); *Sacred Hearts* (BBC Radio 4).

Tom Hughes Fritz

Tom graduated from RADA in 2008.

Film includes: *Cemetery Junction* (Sony Pictures) and the BAFTA nominated *Sex & Drugs & Rock & Roll* (DJ Films).

TV includes: *Casualty 1909* (Stone City Films); *Trinity* (Roughcut).

Sweet Nothings is Tom's professional theatre debut.

Jack Laskey Theodore

Theatre includes: *As You Like It, A New World – A Life of Thomas Paine, In Extremis, Antony and Cleopatra* (Shakespeare's Globe); *The Tragedy of Thomas Hobbes, The Merchant of Venice, The Taming of the Shrew* (RSC); *The Masque of the Red Death* (Punchdrunk); *Hamlet* (Haymarket Theatre Basingstoke); *Biloxi Blues* (Couch Potato Productions); *Hamlet* (Old Vic); *Romeo and Juliet* (Vienna's English Theatre).

Film, TV and Radio includes: *Spilt Milk* – also co-writer (Fifty Nine Productions); *Heartbeat* (ITV); *A Family Portrait* (Fifty Nine Productions); *Arcadia* (BBC Radio 4).

David Sibley Weiring

Theatre includes: *Uncle Vanya* (Young Vic); *Dallas Sweetman* (Paines Plough/ Canterbury Cathedral); *Little Eagles* (RSC); *Rabbit* (Frantic Assembly); *Lear* (Sheffield Crucible); *Cruel and Tender* (Young Vic); *Dirty Wonderland* (Frantic Assembly); *King Lear* (Almeida); *Some Explicit Polaroids* (Out of Joint); *Naked* (Almeida).

Film and TV includes: *Midsomer Murders* (ITV); *Wallander* (BBC); *Land Girls* (BBC); *Mr Nice; Heartless.*

Andrew Wincott Gentleman

Theatre includes: *Lloyd George Knew My Father* (Theatre Royal Bath); *Jane Eyre* (New Farnham Repertory); *Twelfth Night, As You Like It & Sleuth* (Perth Theatre); *Anna Karenina* (Chester); *The Rivals* (Vienna's English Theatre); *Tartuffe, A View From the Bridge, The Aspern Papers & Lost in Yonkers* (Colchester); *Othello* (Theatre Clwyd); *The Green Parakeet* (Greenwich Studio).

TV and Radio includes: *New Tricks* (BBC); *The Archers* (BBC Radio 4).

Luc Bondy Direction

Luc Bondy was born in Zurich in 1948. After graduating from Jacques Lecoq's school, he debuted as a director at Théâtre Universitaire International in Paris where he successfully adapted a novella by Witold Gombrowicz for the stage.

Theatre includes: *Die See*, Edward Bond (Residenztheater München, 1973); *Kalldewey Farce*, Botho Strauss (Schaubühne Berlin, 1982); *Triumph der Liebe*, Marivaux (Schaubühne Berlin, 1985); *Die Stunde da wir nichts voneinander wussten*, Peter Handke (Schaubühne Berlin/Festival d'Automne à Paris, 1994); *Jouer avec le feu*, August Strindberg (Théâtre Vidy Lausanne/Wiener Festwochen, 1996); *En attendant Godot*, Samuel Beckett (Théâtre Vidy Lausanne/Wiener Festwochen, 1998); *Die Möwe*, Anton Chekhov (Burgtheater Wien/Wiener Festwochen, 2000); *Auf dem Land*, Martin Crimp (Schauspielhaus Zürich/Berliner Ensemble, 2001); *Anatol*, Arthur Schnitzler (Burgtheater Wien/Wiener Festwochen, 2002); *Une pièce espagnole*, Yasmina Reza (Théâtre de la Madeleine, Paris/Wiener Festwochen, 2004); *Cruel and Tender*, Martin Crimp (Young Vic co-production with Wiener Festwochen, 2004); *Viol*, Botho Strauss (Odéon-Théâtre de l'Europe, Paris/Wiener Festwochen, 2005); *Schlaf*, Jon Fosse (Burgtheater Wien/Wiener Festwochen, 2006); *König Lear*, William Shakespeare (Burgtheater/Wiener Festwochen, 2007); *La Seconde Surprise de l'amour*, Marivaux (Théâtre Vidy-Lausanne/Théâtre Nanterre-Amandiers/Festival d'Automne à Paris/Wiener Festwochen 2008 a.o.); *Die Zofen*, Jean Genet (Wiener Festwochen/ Volksbühne am Rosa-Luxemburg-Platz, Berlin, 2008).

Opera includes: *Salome*, Richard Strauss (Salzburger Festspiele, 1992); *Don Carlos*, Giuseppe Verdi (Théâtre du Châtelet, Paris, 1996); *The Turn of the Screw*, Benjamin Britten (Festival d'Aix-en-Provence/Wiener Festwochen, 2001); *Hercules*, Georg Friedrich Handel (Festival d'Aix-en-Provence, co-production with Opéra National de Paris, Wiener Festwochen, 2004); *Julie*, Philippe Boesmans (De Munt/La Monnaie, Brüssel, co-production with Wiener Festwochen, Festival d'Aix-en-Provence, 2005); *Idomeneo*, Mozart (Teatro alla Scala, Milan/Operá National de Paris/Teatro Real, Madrid, 2005); *Yvonne, Princesse de Bourgogne*, Witold Gombrowicz (Opera National de Paris/Wiener Festwochen, La Monnaie/De Munt, Brussels, 2009); *Tosca*, Puccini (Metropolitan Opera New York/Teatro alla Scala, Milan, Bayerische Staatsoper, Munich, 2009).

Films: *Die Ortliebschen Frauen* based on a novel by Franz Nabl; *Das weite Land*, Arthur Schnitzler (1986); *Ne fais pas ça!*, (Les films du Lendemain Paris and Net Entertainment Berlin, 2003).

Credits as an author include: *Wo war ich?* (short stories) and in 2009 his first novel *Am Fenster*.

Karl-Ernst Herrmann Set and Light

He was the formative designer at the Schaubühne Berlin; working in close partnership with Peter Stein with whom he has collaborated throughout his career including Stein's famous productions of *Summerfolk* and *As You Like It*. His style has influenced many of the great European directors. He has worked frequently with Luc Bondy and has directed and designed his own opera productions for Brussels Théâtre de la Monnaie, the Wiener Festwochen, the Salzburg Festival, the Vienna State Opera and the Netherlands Opera.

Moidele Bickel Costumes

A long time collaborator of Peter Stein, Moidele was Costume Designer at the Schaubühne Berlin from 1970 – 1992. She was nominated for an Academy Award for Costume Design for Patrice Chéreau's film *La Reine Margot* in 1994 and won a British Academy Award for *La Marquise d'O* by Éric Rohmer. Previous productions with Luc Bondy include: *The Turn of the Screw* (Aix Festival) and *Don Carlos* (Le Théâtre du Châtelet). She recently designed the costumes for David Harrower's *Blackbird* and Michael Haneke's 2009 film *The White Ribbon*.

Gareth Fry Sound

Gareth trained at the Central School of Speech & Drama in theatre design.

Recent work includes: *The Cat in the Hat* (NT & Young Vic); *Babel* (Stan Won't Dance); *Pains of Youth* (NT); *Endgame* (Complicité); *The Fahrenheit Twins* (Told by an Idiot).

Other work includes: *Shun-kin, Noise of Time, Strange Poetry* (Complicité); *Be Near Me & Black Watch* (National Theatre of Scotland); *Othello* (Frantic Assembly); *Tangle, The Swing Left, Zero Degrees and Drifting* (Unlimited Theatre); *Astronaut* (Theatre O); *How Much is Your Iron?, The Jewish Wife* (Young Vic Brecht Fest); *Waves, A Matter of Life and Death* (NT); *Macbeth* (OOJ); *Dancing at Lughnasa* (Old Vic); *The Watery Part of the World* (Sound&Fury).

Geoffrey Layton Dramaturg

As Dramaturg with Luc Bondy: *Das weite Land, En attendant Godot* (Théâtre Vidy-Lausanne); *Wintermärchen* (La Monnaie, Brussels); *The Turn of the Screw* (Festival d'Aix en Provence); *Auf dem Land* (Schauspielhaus Zürich); *Die Möwe, Anatol* ((Burgtheater Wien/Wiener Festwochen); *Ne fais pas ça, Une Piece Espagnole* (Théâtre de la Madeleine); Geoff worked with Karl-Ernst and Ursel Herrmann in La Monnaie, Brussels, and with Peter Zadek in Burgtheater and Münchner Kammerspiele. He has directed *Don Carlos* (Stralsund, Germany); *Combattimento* by Monteverdi and *Orfeo* by Haydn (Nationale Reis Opera).

Eva Dessecker Associate Costume Designer

Studied Art History and Archaeology in Freiburg im Breisgau and has lived in Berlin since 1982. She was assistant and co-worker for Moidele Bickel at the Schaubühne Berlin. At the Salzburg Festival in 1992 she was costume designer for the opera *Aus einem Totenhaus* directed by Klaus Michael Grüber. In 1993 followed *Das Gleichgewicht* by Botho Strauss. Working with Luc Bondy, and set designer Karl-Ernst Herrman.

Eva Maria Dessecker worked in close cooperation with Klaus Michael Grüber on *Splendid* by Jean Genet and *Katharina Von Siena* at the Schaubühne Berlin and Piccolo Theatre Milan in 1994. Other productions include *Bleiche Mutter, Zarte Schwester* by Jorge Semprun, Kunstfest Weimar 1995, *Roberto Zucco* by Bernard-Marie Koltès at the Burgtheater Vienna/Wiener Festwochen in 2001 and *Il Ritorno D; Ulisse in Patria, Idomeneo, Katerian Ismailowa* and *Doctor Faust* at Zurich Opera.

In the 2009/2010 season she designed the costumes for *Die Meistersinger von Nürnberg* for Opera Graz as well as for the National Theatre Weimar set and costumes for Schiller's *Don Carlos*, directed by Felix Ensslin.

Barbara Pral Assistant Design

Trained at the Studium an der Hochschule at the "Mozarteum" in Salzburg. Since training has worked as Assistant Costume and Set Designer for theatre and opera. Her latest design of *Louise* was at the Deutsche Oper am Rhein in Düsseldorf and was directed by Christof Loy.

The Young Vic

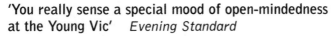

'Thank God for the Young Vic'
The Observer

'You really sense a special mood of open-mindedness at the Young Vic'   *Evening Standard*

Our shows   We present the widest variety of classics, new plays, forgotten works and music theatre. We tour and co-produce extensively within the UK and internationally.

Our artists   Our shows are created by some of the world's great theatre people alongside the most adventurous of the younger generation. This fusion makes the Young Vic one of the most exciting theatres in the world.

Our audience   is famously the youngest and most diverse in London. We encourage those who don't think theatre is 'for them' to make it part of their lives. We give 10% of our tickets to schools and neighbours irrespective of box office demand, and keep prices low.

Our partners near at hand   Each year we engage with 10,000 local people – individuals and groups of all kinds including schools and colleges – by exploring theatre on and off stage. From time to time we invite our neighbours to appear on our stage alongside professionals.

Our partners further away   By co-producing with leading theatre, opera, and dance companies from around the world we challenge ourselves and create shows neither partner could achieve alone.

The Young Vic is a company limited by guarantee, registered in England No. 1188209
VAT Registration No. 236 673 348

The Young Vic (registered charity no. 268876) receives public funding from:

The Young Vic Company

Supporting the Young Vic

The Young Vic relies on the generous support of many trusts, companies and individuals to continue our work on and off stage.

For their recent support we thank

Public Funders
Arts Council England
Equalities and Human Rights Commission
Lambeth Borough Council
London Development Agency
Southwark Council

Corporate Supporters
American Airlines
Bupa
Bloomberg
Cadbury Schweppes Foundation
De La Rue Charitable Trust
HSBC Bank plc
J.P. Morgan
KPMG Foundation
London Communications Agency
North Square Capital
The Merlin Entertainment London Eye

The Directors' Circle

Big Cheeses
HgCapital
Ingenious Media
Land Securities

Hot Shots
Bloomberg
Clifford Chance
Slaughter and May
Taylor Wessing LLP

Trust Supporters
The Arimathea Charitable Trust
The City Bridge Trust
City Parochial Foundation
John S Cohen Foundation
Columbia Foundation Fund of the Capital Community Foundation
Dorset Foundation

D'Oyly Carte Charitable Trust
Equitable Charitable Trust
Eranda Foundation
Ernest Cook Trust
Esmee Fairbairn Foundation
Garrick Charitable Trust
Garfield Weston Foundation
Genesis Foundation
Goethe-Institut
Help a London Child
Henry Smith Charity
Jerwood Charitable Foundation
John Ellerman Foundation
John Thaw Foundation
The Limbourne Trust
Man Group plc Charitable Trust
Martin Bowley Charitable Trust
Peter Moores Foundation
Quercus Charitable Trust
Steel Charitable Trust
The Worshipful Company of Grocers

Production Partnership
Tony & Gisela Bloom
Sandy Chalmers
Kay Ellen Consolver & John Storkerson
Eileen Glynn
Mr & Mrs Roderick Jack
Chris & Jane Lucas
Miles Morland
Nadine Majaro & Roger Pilgrim
Anda & Bill Winters

Best Friends
Jane Attias
Chris & Frances Bates
Alex & Angela Bernstein
The Bickertons
Katie Bradford
Sarah Hall
Richard Hardman & Family
Nik Holttum & Helen Brannigan
Suzanne & Michael Johnson
Tom Keatinge
John Kinder & Gerry Downey
Carol Lake
Simon & Midge Palley
Naomi Russell
Charles & Donna Scott
Justin Shinebourne
Richard & Julie Slater
The Tracy Family
Leo & Susan van der Linden
Rob Wallace

Great Friends
Tim & Caroline Clark
Robyn Durie
Maureen Elton
Jenny Hall
Susan Hyland
Tony Mackintosh
Ian McKellen
Barbara Minto
Frank & Helen Neale
Georgia Oetker
Anthony & Sally Salz
Mr & Mrs Bruce R. Snider
Richard Tomkins
Donna & Richard Vinter
Jimmy & Carol Walker

With special thanks to
Martin Schlaff

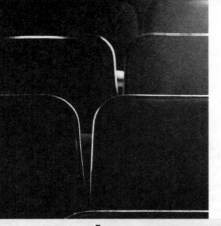

Taylor Wessing

is proud to sponsor

the **Young Vic**

Wiener Festwochen

Luc Bondy is the artistic director of the Wiener Festwochen, one of the world's leading cultural festivals. Juggling traditional and contemporary approaches, the 2010 programme comprises a total of 49 productions with 196 performances, including 6 world premieres and one new production with more than 180,000 visitors. Each year, the Wiener Festwochen creates or collaborates on a series of cultural events presented over six weeks in May and June which combine the highest artistic standards with socially relevant issues and objectives.

The Wiener Festwochen is not only a mirror of the city's enthusiasm for culture but also faces outwards towards other cultures and spheres. The programme of the festival for 2010 provides an overview of the impressive panorama of today's international theatre. Artistic variety is what it's all about. The programme includes operas, concerts, plays, and performances. Artists and ensembles from 23 countries from Argentina, Austria, Belgium, Bosnia, Brazil, Canada, Croatia, Democratic Republic of the Congo, Estonia, France, Germany, Great Britain, Hungary, Iran, Italy, Japan, Latvia, Netherlands, Poland, Russia, Serbia, South Africa and the USA present their views of the world.

The Wiener Festwochen were established in 1951. Since its foundation, the festival has been an integral part of the city's cultural agenda and seems to belong to it more than ever today. A high point of the cultural year, the Wiener Festwochen has become a fixture: a metropolitan festival which focuses on special issues and, by including the artistic practice in other European cities and the world at large, not only presents outstanding achievements but also supports and highlights Viennese creativity.

For further information in English see www.festwochen.at

Giving a voice
to young talent

Land Securities is proud to sponsor the Young Vic

Ruhrfestspiele Recklinghausen

During the Festival time from May 1st to the middle of June, Recklinghausen annually turns into a downright international cultural metropolis. The Ruhrfestspiele are one of the oldest and biggest theatre festivals in Europe. In and around the Ruhrfestspielhaus productions of well-known directors, performances of price-winning actors and presentations of young talents of the theatre scene are connecting to a coherent concept.

In 2005 Dr. Frank Hoffmann assumed the management of the Ruhrfestspiele. "Quality for all" is his conceptual idea, which aims to attract theatre enthusiasts as well as first-time visitors. Every year, the Festival Manager focuses on a selected author respectively and a main theme. Extraordinary projects will furthermore contribute to the success of Capital of Culture in the year of 2010.

With regards to the focus of the programme, Hoffmann places a high value on the involvement of debut performances and premieres. Therefore Recklinghausen annually turns into a "creative place" which invents itself over and over again. With the presentation of co-productions of the Ruhrfestspiele in German and international theatres the festival has an impact far beyond the borders of the region. The exciting readings of famous actors as well as the comedy programme, which presents well-established stars as well as new talents of the genre, enjoy great popularity. Furthermore international artists present extraordinary off-scene performances within the Fringe-Festival. More than 80,000 visitors in 2009 prove the ability of the ambitious festival to present quality while reaching a broad audience at the same time.

The prelude of the festival is the traditional culture folk festival on May 1st, which draws up to 100,000 visitors to the park around the Ruhrfestspielhaus.

warwick arts centre

Warwick Arts Centre is one of the largest arts centres in the UK, attracting around 280,000 visitors a year to over 2,000 individual events embracing music, drama, dance, comedy, literature, films and the visual arts. Situated at the heart of the campus of the University of Warwick in Coventry, the centre is integral to the cultural life of the University and the region and, with seven outstanding spaces on the same site - a concert hall, two theatres, a cinema, gallery, a public lecture space (alongside rehearsal, workshop and creative spaces), it is a unique facility.

The artistic programme is a combination of curated festivals, commissions and presented work which is unashamedly contemporary, balancing the interests and ambitions of audiences and artists so that the contemporary arts are a part of the everyday life for as many people as possible.

The University of Warwick is one of the UK's leading research universities and owns and manages Warwick Arts Centre.

Warwick Arts Centre
The University of Warwick, Coventry, UK

www.warwickartscentre.co.uk

Arthur Schnitzler
Sweet Nothings

a new version by
DAVID HARROWER

faber and faber

First published in 2010
by Faber and Faber Limited
74–77 Great Russell Street
London WC1B 3DA

Typeset by Country Setting, Kingsdown, Kent CT14 8ES
Printed in England by CPI Bookmarque, Croydon, Surrey

A CIP record for this book
is available from the British Library

978-0-571-26892-4

2 4 6 8 10 9 7 5 3 1

Characters

Christine

Katharina

Mizi

Fritz

Theodore

Weiring

Gentleman

SWEET NOTHINGS

Act One

Fritz's elegant room. Fritz asleep, sprawled on a chair.
He wakes.
  Theodore. He holds two letters.

Fritz What are you so happy about?

Theodore Happy to be alive . . . Couple of letters for you.

Fritz Hm . . . My father. And Lensky.

Theodore What's the old man got to say for himself then?

Fritz (*changes the subject*) She's told me . . . She's got it
into her head that . . .

Theodore What?

Fritz She's having second thoughts.

Theodore My prayers are answered. Reason being?

Fritz She won't say. I think it's the jitters. Her conscience
finally deciding to make itself known . . .

Theodore Then your affair is doomed. As soon as their –

Fritz She thinks we're being watched.

Theodore Being *watched*?

Fritz I can't talk her out of it. It's taken root in her head.
(*At the window.*) Over there. On the corner. She thinks
someone watches the apartment.

Theodore Who? His driver? His manservant? *Him?*

Fritz Could you recognise anyone from this distance?

  Theodore looks out.

Theodore Barely. But then no one's there at the moment.

Fritz I tell her don't be stupid, you're hallucinating – she gets upset. We just sit here. She doesn't want to go home, won't take a step outside – if I open the door, she starts panicking – tears . . . This morning she told me she wants us to die together . . .

Theodore Not really what you want to hear . . .

Fritz I went outside to prove it to her. Crossed the street. Casually. As if I was running an errand. No one. Unless the ground swallowed him up.

Theodore A doorway, an entrance hall?

Fritz I checked.

Theodore Must have looked like a very convincing errand.

Fritz It's nothing. She's . . . The fear of getting caught.

Theodore Maybe there's a lesson there . . . Be on your bloody guard . . . She did leave?

Fritz glances over the letter from his father.

Fritz Carriage to the door. Umbrella up . . . My father wants me to go out to the estate after Easter – for a week.

Theodore Only a week? I'd send you for six months. Do you the world of good. Think of all the distractions – horseriding, fresh country air, dairy maids with big milky tits . . .

Fritz It's not a dairy farm . . . If I go would you come with me?

Theodore Can't.

Fritz Why not?

Theodore My exams . . .? They're quite important, so I should try and pass them. I could spare a day or two, I suppose.

Fritz Don't put yourself out.

Theodore But you should definitely go. It'll buck you up. I saw it today, out in the fresh air, riding your horse, you were your old self again. Almost likeable.

Fritz Thank you, dear Theo.

Theodore We get back into town, and within minutes you're back to being Friedrich Nietzsche again. I mean, can you not just stop, Fritz? Stop moping. Stop brooding over that bloody woman.

Fritz At dinner with them last night, it was all smiles and chit-chat and please, have more wine . . . He hasn't a clue.

Theodore You're not planning on doing anything stupid? Anything dangerous?

Fritz Like what?

Theodore Running off with her.

Fritz No. No plans.

Theodore I've put the idea in your head now . . . Finish with her.

Fritz Finish with her?

Theodore I know it's hard for you to break things off with women but . . . An affair you're having shouldn't have *me* on edge . . . You see, you've gone to that place again. Unreachable. What are you thinking?

Fritz There *are* other dangers.

Theodore What about Christine?

Fritz Hm?

Theodore Mizi's friend. The girl I found for you. What's wrong with her?

Fritz You *found* her for me?

9

Theodore She didn't turn up by accident.

Fritz She's a sweet girl.

Theodore Straightforward. And very pretty. Mizi did what was asked of her.

Fritz It would be a change. No histrionics . . .

Theodore That's what you need. A change. Exactly. Some new blood. Uncomplicated. Women who fascinate us should be banned. They have no right being fascinating. Who has the time? Be like me. Start it. Enjoy it. Finish it. No big scenes or tragic, operatic complications. Wham bam, thank you, ma'am.

Fritz You may well have a point, Theo. Crudely expressed but still a point.

Theodore Women are perfectly happy, perfectly within their right, to be ordinary. Ordinary, everyday, unremarkable. But what do men continually do? Make them into either angels or devils. Sometimes both . . . She couldn't stop gazing at you on Tuesday night. What did you *do* to her?

Fritz We talked.

Theodore What was she like?

Fritz At talking? Very competent.

Theodore Because if she's anything like Mizi . . .

Doorbell rings.

Fritz Who's that?

Theodore I'll go. Your face . . .! Oh God, what if it's . . . What if it's *him*? . . . It's them. The girls.

Fritz Christine?

Theodore And Mizi. Round two.

Fritz You invited them here?

Theodore This is the thanks I get . . .

Fritz (*heads towards door*) I sent the servant home.

Theodore Damn, it'll just be the four of us then . . .

Mizi. Fritz after her. She carries a package.

Mizi I hope we're welcome. Theo invited us . . .

Theodore Where's Christine? I told you to bring her.

Mizi She won't be long. Hello, Dori.

Fritz Of course you're welcome. There's just one thing the master planner's overlooked . . .

Theodore I never overlook anything.

He takes the package from Mizi.

You got everything?

Mizi Course I did.

Theodore Any of my money left?

Mizi None. (*To Fritz.*) Where shall I put this?

Fritz Sideboard's fine.

Mizi I bought a little something extra.

Theodore Give Fritz your hat. Come on, the suspense is killing me.

Mizi Cognac, one bottle of.

Theodore She's got the right idea.

Fritz Christine is coming?

Mizi She'll be on the tram now. She was walking her father to the theatre. His sister's just died – her aunt. She was an old maid – lived with them for ever.

Theodore He plays the double bass.

Mizi He plays the violin.

Theodore I thought it was the double bass.

Mizi laughs.

What's funny?

Mizi He's small but he's not that small.

Theodore Who cares about the orchestra? All the action's on stage . . . You could be on the stage.

Mizi I know.

Theodore Turn around. Right round.

Mizi twirls.

Look at me. I approve.

Mizi I knew you would. (*To Fritz.*) I love your apartment. What can you see from the window?

Theodore (*amused*) All sorts of things. Strange men lurking . . .

Mizi I said the same about you before you came over and introduced yourself. Christine, there's a strange man looking at us.

Theodore It made your night.

Mizi He always loved himself?

Fritz It looks onto the Strohgasse. And from next door –

Theodore Fritz. Dull. (*Indicates Mizi.*) A vision in front of him and he wants to describe the view . . .

Mizi I'll drink to that. If I had a drink.

Theodore Coming up.

He gets up, pours drinks.

(*To Mizi.*) How's your mother? How's her toothache?

Mizi Even worse.

Theodore Can't you send her to the dentist?

Mizi She went. He said it was rheumatism. Another thing to complain about.

Theodore They should boil her down to make glue.

Mizi looks at him, hurt.

What?

Mizi You have so many nice things, Fritz.

She looks at a uniform hanging on a dummy.

I love the dragoons' uniform. Were you yellow or black brigade?

Theodore She knows her stuff.

Fritz Yellow.

Mizi My favourite. You're in the reserves now?

Fritz (*nods*) A lieutenant.

Theodore Look at her. Mizi, watch the furniture. Don't get it wet.

Mizi I love the fur-trimmed uniform the reserves wear . . . I bet you look every inch the soldier in it.

Theodore I was in the dragoons too. And I'm in the reserves.

Mizi You never told me that.

Theodore I want to be loved for my own sake.

Mizi Next time we go out, will you both wear your uniforms?

Theodore You'll have to wait until August – weapons training.

Mizi August . . . ?

Theodore Too long to wait?

Mizi You'll be done with us by August . . .

Theodore Just so you know, I'm a much better shot than he is.

Mizi (*to Fritz*) Why did you stand us up yesterday? After the theatre. Don't pretend you don't know.

Fritz (*to Theodore*) You didn't pass on my message?

Theodore Of course I did.

Mizi If an arrangement's been made, you should honour it, Lieutenant.

Fritz Believe me, I'd much rather have been with you. I couldn't get away.

Mizi We could see you from the gods, you know. Sitting behind a lady in a black velvet dress.

Fritz She and her husband wanted to go on somewhere afterwards. I couldn't get away.

Mizi You couldn't sit still . . .

Fritz What do you mean?

Mizi Shifting about, looking around you. I said to Christine, why sit in a box if you don't want to be seen? It looked like torture.

Fritz I don't like people spying on me.

Mizi I don't care what you do. But Christine . . . She's not like me. That's all I'll say.

Fritz Good, because you've said enough.

The doorbell rings.

Mizi The woman herself.

Fritz exits.

Theodore Do me a favour, will you?

Mizi Depends.

Theodore Never bring up anything else we do . . . And no one wants to hear about your military campaigns.

Mizi Well, you're one now, aren't you?

Theodore Open your legs.

Mizi No.

Theodore Open them. Wider.

Mizi Can I get the same again, please?

Fritz and Christine. She carries flowers.

Christine Good evening, Theodore.

Theodore (*about flowers*) You really shouldn't have.

Christine (*to Fritz*) You don't mind us coming here?

Fritz (*about Theodore*) I've forgiven him.

Mizi What took you so long?

Christine (*to Mizi*) I got held up by Katharina.

Mizi Oh God . . .

Fritz Who?

Mizi Not someone you're likely to know. Any woman younger than her has no right to be.

Christine She's always been very good to me.

Mizi This one never thinks bad of anyone. What's wrong with you?

Christine These are for you.

She gives Fritz the flowers. He holds them awkwardly.

They'll need water.

Fritz (*looks around*) A vase . . .

Theodore No, not a vase . . .

He takes the flowers, plucking the petals off.

We need to have them fluttering from the ceiling onto your pretty heads.

Fritz Give me them.

Fritz finds a vase, puts them in. He puts Christine's jacket and hat on a chair.

Mizi Spring and it's getting dark already.

Fritz I'll light a lamp.

Theodore No, we'll have candles. (*To Mizi.*) Up. Help me.

He and Mizi light the candles on the chest, desk and sideboard.

Fritz Are you well?

Christine Better now . . . I've been dying to see you.

Fritz We saw each other yesterday.

Christine From a distance. We weren't together. I should be annoyed with you . . .

Fritz I've already been told off about that. I was with people; I couldn't get away.

Christine Who were they?

Fritz Friends. Acquaintances.

Christine And the lady in the black velvet dress?

Fritz I can't remember what anyone was wearing.

Christine That's nice to know.

Fritz Sometimes I can. I remember meeting a young woman a few weeks ago – very pretty – wearing a dark grey blouse . . . And yesterday she was wearing a jacket, a black and white jacket.

Christine (*indicates her jacket*) Like this?

Fritz Identical. I like that locket.

Christine You said that last time. That's why I wear it. Do you think about me?

Fritz Do I think about you?

Christine I think about you.

Theodore Of course he thinks about you. He told me himself. Don't you?

Fritz Yes.

Theodore He's always asking about you.

Christine I liked walking in the park with you.

Fritz All those children playing tig. Pointless game.

Christine Thinking about is never as good as seeing – do you agree?

Fritz I do agree.

Christine I want to see more of you.

Fritz Then we should try and arrange that. But not too much.

Christine Not *too* much?

Fritz No.

Christine Why not?

Fritz Because . . . Because I may have to go away for a few weeks.

Christine Where?

Fritz I didn't say I was. I might want to, though.

Christine You might want to go away for a few weeks?

Fritz To be on my own for a while. I have these moods and . . . Don't you ever feel like that? You just want to . . .

Christine I never have those kinds of moods.

Fritz How can you say that?

Christine You know, for you I'd . . . There will never be a time I don't want to see you. Ever.

Fritz Don't talk like that. I hate all that grand, sweeping . . . For ever and ever, my one and only true love . . .

The candles are lit.

Theodore You think you two could tear yourselves away from each other and take a look at my artistry?

Fritz Theo, you're a genius.

Theodore Anyone hungry? 'Cause I bloody am.

Mizi And me. (*To Christine.*) Come and help me.

Fritz I'll show you where everything is.

Mizi Tablecloth first.

Fritz That drawer there.

Mizi No.

Fritz The next one?

She opens it. No tablecloth. She opens another, finds one.

Mizi Ah.

Theodore Reminds me of the cabaret. That woman dancing.

Christine I remember someone promising to take us to the cabaret.

Theodore This one is 'men only', sweetheart.

Mizi Can't really compare with a black velvet dress . . .

Fritz What's this fascination with the black velvet dress?

Mizi Cutlery?

Fritz The knives are already out.

He opens the cutlery drawer in the sideboard.

Mizi Plates? Thank you. We can manage by ourselves now.

Theodore stretches out on the divan. Fritz joins him as Mizi and Christine lay the table.

Theodore My boots needs polishing when you're finished over there.

Mizi Have you seen Fritz in his uniform?

Christine No.

Mizi You should. I'm sure he looks magnificent.

They continue talking.

Theodore I'm pretty sure this is what heaven will feel like . . .

Mizi Is there any coffee in the machine?

Fritz There should be . . . Can you light the spirit lamp? That machine takes years to make the coffee.

Theodore She's a tiger. A tigress. I've scratches everywhere. (*Indicates Christine.*) Look at her. How can you compare her with a man's wife? So young. So enthusiastic. Full of the joys of the world.

Fritz You can't compare them. They're so different.

Theodore You know our problem?

Fritz No – but I feel sure you're going to tell me . . .

Theodore Our problem is: we can't *stand* the women we fall in love with.

Fritz Is that right?

Theodore We should tell them we love them – then stay away from them. Never see them. Spend all our time with women we're completely indifferent about. So much more rewarding . . .

Fritz laughs.

Mizi What was that? Tell us.

Theodore Nothing for your ears. I was ruminating. Imparting wisdom.

Mizi I'd love to hear that.

Theodore (*to Fritz*) I keep telling myself this is the last time, this will be absolutely the last night I see her, but then . . . It's so damn good I keep going back for more.

Christine Where do you keep your dessert spoons?

Fritz (*returns to sideboard*) Here.

Mizi goes to Theodore, runs her fingers through his hair. Fritz opens the package that Mizi brought with her. He lays out tins of sardines, cold meats, butter, cheese.

Theodore My furry tigress . . .

Fritz You brought so much . . .

Christine So you won't tell me?

Fritz Tell you what?

Christine The black velvet dress?

Fritz Will you stop asking me? (*More gently.*) I told you at the start: no questions. That's why I like being with you. The world outside disappears. I never ask you questions.

Christine You can ask me whatever you want.

Fritz I don't want to.

Mizi (*approaches*) What are you doing . . . ?

She takes the food from Fritz, puts it on plates.

Theodore Fritz, we need more drink.

Fritz I'll see what I can find.

He goes into the adjoining room.

Theodore (*surveys the table*) Beautifully laid, ladies . . .

Mizi (*to Christine*) Imagine being waited on hand and foot your whole life . . .

Theodore Pity you'll never know . . .

Fritz (*enters carrying several bottles*) I found a few bottles.

Mizi The roses . . .! We forgot the roses!

She takes the roses from the vase, climbs onto a chair, scatters them over the table.

Christine Watch you don't fall.

Theodore Not on the plates – we're eating off them . . .

Mizi climbs onto the table.

Christine Mizi . . .

Mizi I want to get the right effect.

Theodore You too.

Christine No. (*To Fritz.*) Sorry.

Mizi What a view you get up here.

Theodore Same down here.

Christine Mizi, get down.

Theodore Mizi, stay up!

Mizi A hand, please.

Fritz holds out his hand. Mizi takes it, steps down.

Thank you, Lieutenant. Such bravery.

Theodore Corkscrew. We demand a corkscrew.

Fritz There.

Mizi tries to open a bottle of wine.

I'll do that.

Theodore For God's sake, let me do it.

He takes the bottle and corkscrew from Fritz.

You can give us a bit of the old . . . (*Indicates piano.*)

Mizi Yes. Play something for us.

She goes to the piano, opens it.

Fritz (*to Christine*) You want me to?

Christine I'd love to hear you.

Fritz (*going to piano*) You play after me, agreed?

Christine I'm not that good.

Mizi Listen to her . . . She plays beautifully. Sings as well.

Fritz You never told me that.

Christine You never asked me.

Fritz Did you study singing?

Christine My father taught me – but I don't have much of a voice.

Mizi She's telling lies.

Christine Since my aunt died, we don't sing like we used to.

Fritz What do you do during the day?

Christine I help my father. I sew. I copy out scores.

Fritz Musical scores?

Christine What other kind of scores are there?

Theodore And what are the *scales* of pay for that?

The others laugh.

Mizi If I had her voice, I'd be a star of the stage.

Theodore You wouldn't need your voice, you've other talents . . . And what do you do all day apart from climbing on furniture?

Mizi Oh, absolutely nothing, I just feed and dress my two younger brothers in the morning before taking them both to school and then I bring them back at the end of the day and do their homework with them in the evening. My mother's right, I don't know what hard work is.

Theodore Is that right? Is she telling the truth?

Mizi I also worked in a shop until last autumn, eight in the morning until eight at night.

Theodore What kind of shop was it?

Mizi A milliner's.

Theodore I take my hat off to you.

Mizi My mother's insisting I go back to it.

Theodore Why did you leave?

Mizi It wasn't the hats. It was the people under them.

Fritz (*to Christine*) Come and sing something for us.

Theodore No, food first, music later.

Fritz (*stands*) Allow me.

He leads her to the table, pulls out a chair for her to sit.

Mizi The coffee . . . ! It's boiling over.

Theodore Forget about it.

Mizi But it's boiling over.

She blows out the spirit lamp. They sit down at the table. Fritz pours out the wine.

Theodore No cakes, Mizi, they're for after.

Mizi After what?

Theodore (*raises his glass*) Cheers.

Mizi To your health. And to your wealth.

Theodore (*gets to his feet*) Ladies and gentlemen, it's my great honour to introduce . . . Damn. Sorry. Wrong occasion.

Mizi I love it when people make speeches at dinner.

Theodore Ladies and gentlemen, sitting here, the groom may look innocent enough but my God, if you only knew . . . Oh. Sorry. Wrong again.

Mizi I have a cousin who always makes speeches in verse.

Theodore Which regiment does he serve with?

Mizi Be quiet. He makes every line rhyme, he's . . .

Theodore Every line rhyme? That must take some time. It'd make me want to climb. The walls . . .

Fritz Why's nobody drinking? Christine.

They clink glasses.

Theodore (*clinks glass with Mizi*) To the old men who speak in rhyme.

Mizi To the young men who never say a word. (*A glance at Fritz.*) To the four of us, to me and Theo, to you and Christine . . .

Theodore To our evening. However it may end. And for now, may it never.

Mizi For now, may it never.

Fritz kisses Mizi. Theodore tries to kiss Christine. She shrinks back.

Christine (*smiles*) No . . .

Theodore Yes. Or it's bad luck the rest of our days.

He kisses her.

There.

Mizi It's so hot in here.

Theodore She never says that when I kiss her.

Fritz It's the candles.

Mizi And the wine.

Theodore Lean over and try the *pièce de résistance*. And have some cake as well.

He cuts some cake, puts it into her mouth.

Taste good?

Mizi Delicious. Mizi want more.

Theodore Does she now? Fritz, I think it's time . . . to play for us. What did you think I meant?

Fritz You're sure?

Christine Yes, play for us.

Mizi Something to put us in the mood.

Theodore fills the glasses.

No more for me.

But she drinks more anyway.

Christine This wine's so strong.

Theodore (*points to the wine*) Fritz, drink! It loosens the fingers.

Fritz drains his glass. He goes to the piano.

Mizi Play the 'Double Eagle'.

Fritz How does that go again?

Mizi Theo, do you know the 'Double Eagle'?

Theodore I can't play or sing or hum a note.

Fritz I know it, but it's not coming to me.

Mizi (*sings*) La . . . la . . . la . . .

Fritz I've got it.

He plays, but it's not right.

Mizi No, like this . . . Watch, one finger.

She plays the piano with one finger.

Fritz Yes. Yes.

He plays. She sings along with him.

Theodore A military march. That brings back memories.

Mizi Same here.

Fritz (*gets it wrong again, stops*) I can't. I don't have a good enough ear.

Mizi You have a lovely ear. Christine's always talking about your ear.

Christine Stop it.

Fritz starts to improvise.

Mizi (*after a few bars*) Stop, stop. That's awful.

Fritz I wrote it myself.

Mizi You can't even dance to it.

Fritz Depends how you dance.

Theodore Come on. Let's try.

*He takes her by the waist. They start to dance.
Christine watches them. Theodore presses into Mizi,
who responds. Theodore guides Mizi towards the door
to the other room.*

Mizi Where are we going?

Theodore You'll see.

Mizi What if I don't want to?

Theodore I don't care what you want.

Mizi Christine, don't just stand there. Help me.

Theodore Too late. You're beyond help.

*They look at each other, kiss. Fritz and Christine
watch them.*

Fritz What should I play to accompany them?

Christine Something loud and brash?

Theodore Something epic.

Mizi Something that doesn't last very long.

Theodore looks at her.

What? Aw . . .

Theodore (*to Fritz*) Can we swap?

Fritz No.

Mizi I want you for myself.

Theodore (*to Fritz*) You sure?

Mizi Leave her alone.

Theodore It's obvious she doesn't want him . . . She's so besotted with me she can't even look at me . . .

Christine There's not much to look at, that's all.

Theodore You hear that?

Fritz Insolence.

Theodore Insurrection. (*To Christine.*) Come here. That's an order . . .

Christine (*to Fritz*) May I?

Fritz nods. Christine sits next to him.

Fritz His men never listened to him either.

Theodore (*looks at them for a moment*) Wine.

He heads for the wine.

Mizi Do you actually enjoy playing the piano or do you have something against it?

Fritz A bad experience when I was young. (*To Christine.*) Would your father accompany me on his violin, d'you think?

Christine I think he would run a mile.

Mizi I just love your uniform. Can I try it on?

Christine Mizi . . .

Mizi Why not?

Fritz You play.

Mizi Why not?

Christine No.

Mizi puts on the uniform.

Fritz I know you'll be better than me.

Christine How do you know?

Fritz I just do. In fact, I think . . .

Christine What?

Fritz I think . . .

Christine Tell me?

Fritz No.

Mizi How do I look?

Christine Tell me . . .

He looks at her, indicates his cheek with his finger. She kisses it.

Fritz I think in just about everything there is – life, morals, manners, bearing, talent, interest, kindness and understanding – you are better than me.

Mizi I feel completely different with this on.

Fritz How do you feel?

Mizi Indestructible.

Theodore Indescribable.

Mizi What was that, Lieutenant? What did you say?

Theodore Nothing, sir.

Mizi Good. My glass needs to be filled.

Theodore Yes, sir. Straight away, sir.

He goes to fill her glass. The wine bottle is empty.

We've run dry, sir.

Mizi Run dry? What kind of shabby outfit are you running here?

Fritz What did she say?

Mizi She called you a shabby outfit . . .

Fritz Did she?

He stands up, lurches a bit.

Theodore We're at war, sir. The wine's not getting through.

Mizi I don't care. The general needs replenishing.

Fritz (*to Christine*) We'll attack her from behind.

Mizi (*laughs*) You'll do no such thing.

Fritz Classic pincer movement.

Mizi What's wrong with my front?

Theodore Your front's covered, that's what's wrong.

He pulls the uniform off her.

That's opened it up a bit.

Fritz I've lost Christine.

Christine I'm right here. The right flank.

Mizi Betrayed. Double-crossed.

Fritz Attack!

Theodore Show no mercy . . . !

Mizi You'll be court-martialled for this, all of you.

Theodore I've got her front! I've captured it!

Fritz Keep hold of it.

They all fall to the floor or onto the sofa.
The Gentleman walks in. They don't notice him at first. He walks around the room, inspecting it. Mizi sees him first.

Mizi Hello. How long have you been there?

The Gentleman says nothing. He seems to be looking for something.

Not very friendly, are you? Theo . . .

No response.

Fritz . . .

Fritz What?

Mizi There's a man in your apartment. I think he's a thief.

The Gentleman flashes her a look. Fritz raises his head. He stares at the Gentleman, dumbfounded. He gets to his feet. Theodore has seen him now, too.

Gentleman Have I disturbed your little get-together?

Mizi (*to Theodore*) Who is he?

Theodore Shut up.

Mizi Yes, you have disturbed it. You should be ashamed.

Theodore Mizi . . .

Gentleman Can I talk to you alone?

Fritz Of course. (*To Christine.*) Could you leave us for a moment?

Christine What's wrong?

Fritz Theo . . . (*Indicates the room downstairs.*)

Theodore Come on.

Christine Where are we going?

Fritz (*to Gentleman*) One moment.

Theodore Mizi, next door.

Mizi I'm comfortable here.

Christine Is everything all right?

Fritz I need to speak with him. I won't be long.

Theodore Mizi . . .

Mizi What is all this? . . . I'm coming. (*To Christine.*) He doesn't want us to be seen.

Theodore They have to talk.

Fritz I won't be long.

Theodore (*to Fritz*) He's trying to trick you. Don't say anything. Don't admit to anything.

Theodore, Mizi and Christine leave. Silence between Fritz and Gentleman.

Theodore Sit down here and keep quiet.

Mizi Why? Who is he?

Theodore It's business. Nothing to do with you. (*He stands apart.*)

Christine Nothing to do with us.

They laugh.

Gentleman A party?

Fritz Sort of.

Mizi Sit down. Shut up.

Gentleman It either is or it isn't.

Fritz Can I ask what you're here for?

The Gentleman rummages through the girls' coats, etc.

Mizi I left my wine in there.

Christine So did I.

Fritz What are you doing?

Gentleman Looking.

Fritz What for?

Mizi and Christine make for the door.

Sir . . .

Mizi You first.

Gentleman She left her veil . . . My wife left her veil here.

Fritz I don't find that funny.

Gentleman Nor do I . . . Do you have it?

They look at each other. Theodore sees the girls.

Theodore Get back in here . . .

Mizi No.

Mizi and Christine appear in the room.

Don't mind us . . .

Christine Sorry. We've lost our wine.

Mizi Have you seen it?

Fritz Here.

He picks up their glasses, gives them to Christine.

Go now. Get out.

Christine Are you angry with me?

Mizi (*to Gentleman*) Are you in the Dragoons? . . .
Doesn't he talk?

Christine Mizi . . .

She takes Mizi out. Theodore pulls them inside.

Theodore For God's sake, what did I say . . .?

Mizi Oh Dori, adorable Dori . . . No one ever listens to you.

Theodore gives her a brief glare, turns away.

Gentleman Do you have it?

Fritz . . . No.

Pause. The Gentleman resumes his search.

I don't have it.

The Gentleman stops. Pause. He pulls out a stack of letters, hundreds; drops them on the floor.

Gentleman These are yours . . . I want hers.

Fritz stares at the letters. The Gentleman shakes with anger.

The letters she wrote to you.

Fritz I have none.

Gentleman Get them . . . All lovers keep letters.

Fritz I have no letters.

Gentleman I don't want them found here, later.

Fritz They won't be.

Pause.

Is there anything else I can do for you?

Gentleman Anything else? (*Laughs.*) Anything else?

Pause.

Fritz I am at your disposal.

Gentleman Good . . .

Fritz My seconds will . . .

Gentleman (*interrupts*) Send them to my house tomorrow. They will be told where and when.

The Gentleman bows, leaves. Fritz stands silently for a few moments.

Fritz Theo . . . (*Louder.*) Theo. Theo!

In the next room, Theodore hears him. Warning glance to the girls. He enters the room.

Theodore Well?

Fritz He knows.

Theodore stares at him, then at the letters on the floor. He picks one up.

Theodore Never send letters.

Fritz It *was* him standing out there . . . Will you help me?

He begins to pick each of the letters up.

You'll be my seconds. You and Lensky.

Theodore I'll go and talk to him. I'll . . .

Fritz It's too late for that.

Theodore Of course it's not.

Fritz It's for the best . . . Lensky – I'll need to talk to him.

Theodore watches him, then starts to pick the letters up alongside Fritz.

Theodore Now?

Fritz Yes. No, not now. Tomorrow – early. He'll be at the coffee-house. Bring him here. Both of you come here.

Theodore We'll come to an agreement, don't worry.

Fritz He should have shot me here. Got it over with.

Theodore We won't agree to his terms – we'll . . .

Fritz You will agree. Whatever the terms are, you'll accept them.

Theodore There's always the possibility you'll kill him . . .

Fritz (*not listening*) She had a premonition. We both did. We somehow knew.

Theodore Stop it. I don't want to hear talk like that.

Fritz goes to the desk, locks away the letters.

Fritz Will you find out what's happened to her? If she's all right?

Theodore I'll do my best.

Fritz But no postponing – promise me.

Theodore But it can't be tomorrow – we need a day at least. And I'll have to clean your bloody pistols, won't I? It'll be all right, I don't know why, I just know it will be.

Fritz (*smiles*) Always rely on Theo . . . He has the right to shoot first . . . What do we tell them?

Theodore Tell them to go.

Fritz No. Let's finish the party. Don't say a word.

Theodore It's none of their business.

Fritz plays a few chords. Theodore knocks on the door.

Are you two hiding in there? I thought you came for a party . . . ?

Mizi and Christine.

Mizi This is ridiculous.

Christine Don't . . .

Mizi We don't get pushed out like . . . lepers.

Christine I'm not a leper.

Mizi Has whoever it was gone?

Christine (*goes over to Fritz*) Who was it?

Fritz (*continues playing*) I knew it! More questions . . .
It was nothing. Business affairs.

Christine Tell me the truth.

Theodore He doesn't have to tell you anything.

Fritz It was nothing.

Mizi Leave him alone, Christine. Let them do what they
want. Let them be mysterious.

Theodore Come here, you, I was dancing with you.
Maestro, music, please.

*Fritz plays. Theodore and Mizi dance. After a few
beats, Mizi falls back into an armchair.*

Mizi I can't dance any more.

*Theodore kisses her, sits on the arm of her chair. Fritz
at the piano with Christine.*

Christine Keep playing.

Fritz (*smiles*) Enough for today.

Christine I wish I could play like you . . .

Fritz How often do you practise?

Christine Not enough. We only have an old upright.

Fritz I'd like to see it.

Christine Nothing like this.

Fritz I don't know anything about you. I want to know more.

Christine There's not a lot to tell. I don't have many secrets . . .

Fritz Have you ever been in love?

She just looks at him.

Does your father know you're here?

Christine No.

Fritz Does your father love you?

Christine I used to tell him everything.

Fritz Everyone needs secrets.

Christine I wish I knew what you thought of me. Deep down.

Fritz You really don't know?

Christine The way you talk to me sometimes, your voice like that . . . I just think of us together. I can't help it.

She leans her head against the piano. Fritz strokes her hair.

Keep doing that. It's nice.

Quiet in the room.

Theodore Any of those cigars left?

Fritz crosses to the sideboard to look for them. Mizi has fallen asleep. Fritz holds out the box.

Fritz How about some coffee?

He pours out two cups.

Theodore Anyone else?

Fritz Mizi?

Theodore Let her sleep, Fritz. Christine, would you . . .?

He indicates she should pour coffee.

You shouldn't be drinking. You need a good night's sleep.

Fritz looks at him, gives a sardonic laugh.

I'm serious.

Fritz I want you to bring Lensky here tonight.

Theodore All right. Mizi, we're going. Wake up.

Mizi (*she wakes*) Do I smell coffee? I want some.

Theodore Come on.

Fritz (*goes to Christine*) Tired?

Christine I blame your wine. I can feel a headache coming on.

Fritz You need some fresh air.

Christine Will you see me home?

Fritz Theo will. I can't. I have to stay here. Sort out a few things.

Christine What?

Fritz (*doesn't reply; after a moment*) I'm exhausted. We were out in the country this morning.

Theodore We'll take you with us next time.

Mizi Only if you both wear your uniforms.

Christine Will we see each other again?

Fritz I'll write to you.

Christine When?

Fritz Tomorrow.

Christine All right. Goodbye.

She turns to go.

Fritz Christine . . . Six o'clock, tomorrow. In the park – beside the tramline.

Christine (*nods*) Six o'clock.

Mizi Are you coming with us?

Theodore No, he's not.

Fritz Take some cake with you, it'll just be left.

Mizi (*to Theodore*) Is that all right, sir? Some cake for us poor girls?

Christine Don't talk like that.

Mizi I'll put the candles out.

She goes round putting the candles out one after the other. The candle on the desk is the only one remaining lit.

Christine Will I open a window? It's so stuffy in here.

She opens the window. Fritz comes to the door, holding the candle to light their way.

Mizi Are the lights out on the stairs?

Theodore Yes.

Christine Smell the fresh air . . .

Mizi Is May spring or summer?

Theodore Come on, move yourselves.

Mizi (*to Fritz*) Thank you. Who knows if we'll meet again.

Theodore Out.

They leave. The door stays open, and their voices are heard from the hall. The apartment door opens.

Theodore Mind the steps.

Mizi Thanks for the cake.

Theodore Shut up, you'll wake the neighbours.

Christine Goodnight.

Theodore Goodnight.

Fritz is heard closing and locking the apartment door. He re-enters, puts the candle on the desk. Downstairs the front door is heard opening and closing.

Christine (*from the street outside*) Goodnight.

Mizi Goodnight, Lieutenant . . .

Theodore For God's sake, will you shut up . . .

Their voices fade. Fritz continues to look out for a few seconds, then sinks into the armchair near the window.

Act Two

*Christine's room. Christine is alone in her underwear.
She hums a song, happy. From far away, the sound of
a waltz. She starts to dance. It becomes wild, euphoric.
Katharina. Who watches her. Frowns.*

Christine Katharina . . .

Katharina You aren't dressed.

Christine No, I'm not.

She laughs, puts clothes on.

Katharina Are you all right?

Christine It's a lovely evening.

Katharina It's to get cold later.

Christine Who says that?

Katharina *I* say. And my husband. It's still spring, you
know. You have to watch spring.

Christine My father's not here.

Katharina I can see that.

Christine There was music . . .

Katharina It's you I was looking for.

Christine I don't have much time.

Katharina You're going out?

Christine I have to hurry.

Katharina Where?

Christine To the park. Six o'clock.

Katharina Why don't you come with us? My husband and I – and Lina – we're going to the concert there. Come. We can all have supper.

Christine I can't.

Katharina Of course you can.

Christine I'd like to but I can't.

Katharina Lina will be disappointed.

Christine Tell her I'm sorry.

Katharina She always asks why you never come and play with her any more and I never know what to tell her. I tried telling her you're too busy – but you can't tell my Lina that – she saw right through that. I see her all the time, she said, going in and out; laughing. She never looks that busy. I don't know when the next concert will be.

Christine Probably next week. They're usually every week.

Katharina Why would you want to come with us anyway? . . . You'll have a better time on your own.

　Christine gives her a look.

Has your father left for the evening?

Christine No, he's coming home first. The show doesn't start until seven thirty.

Katharina Of course – seven thirty. I keep forgetting. Can I wait?

Christine I don't know how long he'll be.

Katharina My husband was wondering whether he could get us tickets. Could he?

Christine You'd have to ask him.

Katharina I hear the show's not doing that well. For audiences. Lovely reviews. No audience.

Christine I think that's the weather. It's been so warm.

Katharina So there will be some tickets. Better we have them than the seats stay empty. I'm always saying we'd never get to go to the theatre if your father didn't live next door. The prices. My husband says it's because they want to keep the likes of us out. That's a lovely dress. The colour suits you. New?

Christine No. Old.

Katharina Well, it looks as good *as* new. You see some wonderful young men at the concerts. So polite, so well turned out. Don't let me hold you up if you're rushing.

Christine I won't.

Katharina Little Lina's face I'm thinking of. My husband too; he'll be disappointed. 'I've almost forgotten what Christine looks like,' he said to me last week.

Christine Tell him the same as I always did . . . I'm quite a topic of conversation amongst you.

Katharina Not us, Christine . . . Other people, yes. We just want to know you're happy . . . You know people round here. Not shy with their opinions.

Christine What are they saying?

Katharina You think I listen to them? . . . Sometimes you pick up little things, you know . . .? And you say, well, *maybe* . . . That could be the case – maybe whoever said that *does* have a point . . .

Christine To be honest, I don't care what they say.

Katharina That's exactly what I told my husband you'd say . . .! Christine doesn't care what they say. She's a grown-up – she does what she wants now.

Christine I'm going now.

Katharina Mustn't be late, eh?

Christine No.

Katharina Best not keep him waiting.

Christine It is a him actually.

Katharina I know it's a him.

Christine How do you know?

Katharina And not really the kind of *him* I was expecting.

Christine Why not just say what you want to say?

Katharina That tone – I've never heard you speak in that tone . . .

Christine Say what you want to say.

Katharina Sweet little Chrissie, where has she gone . . . ?

Christine Please, would you leave now?

Katharina Aren't you the one who's wanting to leave . . . ?

Christine Close the door behind you.

She walks to the door.

Katharina If your father was here . . .

Christine But he's not.

Katharina Be careful.

Christine What does that mean?

Katharina Vienna's a big city, lovely parks, boulevards to walk along, cafés – and you arranged to meet this man only a hundred yards from your front door?

Christine What's wrong with that?

Katharina You need me to tell you?

Christine I can meet who I want. Other girls meet men and . . .

Katharina Other girls do meet men. *Suitable* men . . . When my husband told me, I refused to believe him – it was him that saw you. 'I'm telling you it was her,' he said to me. 'No,' I said, 'it won't have been Christine, not Christine, she's not the kind of girl to go out walking with wealth . . .'

Christine Don't call him that.

Katharina 'Go out walking with . . . smart gentlemen at night – but if she did, if she did go out walking with smart gentlemen at night, surely she'd have more sense than to walk along our street with him, our street with all of its windows which people can see out of . . .' 'Well, go and ask her yourself,' he said. 'And it's hardly surprising,' he said, 'is it? Because she never comes to visit us like she used to do when she was younger; have a glass of milk, slice of cake, tell us what she'd been doing that day. No,' he said, 'instead she'd much rather flit around with that Mizi girl – that Mizi girl who's a bad influence – who's not half the girl Christine is.' I'm only telling you what he said . . . Of course, he didn't call her that Mizi girl, he called her something much worse, much worse than that . . . which I won't repeat. Trollop, he called her. That was it. Men can use such vulgar terms sometimes – but you know, I can see his point. And we both spoke about how kind and caring you'd been with your aunt, God rest her soul. You were her world, you know. And how conscientious and hard-working you've always been; how much you help your father. In fact, my husband said that to Lina – she was there too when were having this conversation – 'Lina,' he said, 'that's how *you* must be when you're older. Like Christine. Like Christine was . . .'

You're sure you don't want to come to the concert? . . .
Does your father know?

Christine is silent.

He has a right to, don't you think?

Weiring. A sprig of lilac in his hand.

Weiring There you are . . . Katharina. You well?

Katharina I was passing. I just dropped in.

Weiring kisses Christine on both cheeks, then again on her forehead. She pulls back slightly at the last kiss.

Christine She wants more free tickets.

Katharina But if there's none, it doesn't matter . . .

Weiring They're not exactly flocking to see us . . . (*To Christine.*) Will you walk me to the theatre? I haven't seen that dress in a while.

Katharina It's an old one.

Weiring You're going out?

Christine I was just leaving.

Weiring I was going to say – what are you doing indoors? Both of you. It's beautiful outside. Heaven. The air's like honey. For you –

The lilac is for Christine.

Christine Lilac.

Katharina Very nice. Very thoughtful.

Weiring All the bushes in the park are in full bloom – you should see the colour of them.

Christine (*indicates sprig, teasing him*) This colour . . .?

Weiring (*smiles*) But everywhere you look. Bush after bush. Alas, Katharina, if I'd known you were here . . .

Katharina So you took it?

Weiring Took what?

Katharina The lilac. You took it from the park?

Weiring Guilty.

Katharina Broke it off the branch . . .

Weiring Snapped it clean off. I couldn't help myself. Officer.

Christine smiles.

Katharina What if the park-keeper had seen you . . .?

Weiring But he didn't.

Katharina But if he had –

Weiring But he didn't.

Katharina But if he had –

Weiring But he didn't.

Christine I'm going now.

Katharina And if everyone thought like that . . .

Weiring Then there'd be chaos, wouldn't there? Societal breakdown . . .

Katharina Just helped themselves . . .

Weiring If you saw them, Katharina, I think even *you* would be tempted. Christine could go with you and keep watch . . .

Katharina I've already asked Christine to come to the park with us but she can't – she's busy.

Weiring You're meeting someone?

Christine Yes.

Weiring No time for her father any more . . .

Katharina No . . .

Weiring I'm old and past it, amn't I, Christine?

Christine Course not.

She kisses him.

Weiring (*he holds on to her*) Will you be long?

Christine I don't know. Maybe.

Weiring Not too late.

Christine leaves. Silence between Katharina and Weiring.

Katharina She's struck up quite a friendship with this Mizi.

Weiring I'm glad. She hasn't had an easy time of it recently.

Katharina Well, none of you have.

Weiring No. (*Beat.*) How's little L—

Katharina (*at the same time*) Not just her. (*Repeats.*) Not just her.

Beat.

Weiring How's Lina? I should take my coat off. Too warm for it . . . Mizi's good for her. She gets out more.

Katharina Why does a girl shorten her name to a sound? Mizi. It sounds like a sneeze. A cat sneezing . . . Where do they both find the money to be out all the time . . . ?

Weiring It's not all the time.

Katharina Lina hears their shoes on the stairs. Clack clack clack. Up and down.

Weiring She sat here the whole winter – for the last three or four years – in that chair, sewing clothes, embroidering. I leave for rehearsals, I get back at night – she's still in that chair. My sister used to always fall asleep across from her and Christine would not have to make a sound . . .

Katharina She can be a thoughtful girl.

Weiring And we eat every night together and after we're done, she sits down again to copy out scores . . . She should be able to enjoy herself every so often.

Katharina How's her singing coming along?

Weiring Good . . . In here, a small room, her voice is good. It's lovely, the tone of it, but . . . it could be stronger. But I love listening to her.

Katharina But it's not a living? . . . She won't be taken on by the theatre?

Weiring No.

Katharina Sad.

Weiring But she knows that. She's clear-eyed, Christine. She won't let herself get disappointed. I thought I could perhaps get her an audition for the chorus . . .

Katharina She's pretty – she'd fit right in. Pays hardly anything though, does it?

Weiring They're not the best voices so it would be like admitting to her she's . . . (*He breaks off.*)

Katharina Lina's almost eleven now. We know what we want for her. (*Pause.*) If Christine had come to the concert, there are young men there, with good prospects. It's where a lot of couples meet. It would be a weight off your mind . . .

Weiring What do you mean?

Katharina I don't think I'm being unclear – am I?

Weiring She's still got so much in front of her . . .

Katharina The father of an eligible young man should be hearing this, not me.

Weiring But to throw her life away . . .

Katharina It's not throwing her life –

Weiring On, what? A shopkeeper or a draper or a . . . (*He stops.*)

Katharina What? What were you going to say? A stocking-maker? Like my husband?

Weiring I didn't mean –

Katharina He may only be stocking-maker but he is a good and honest and upright man who –

Weiring I didn't mean your husband. I meant –

Katharina I threw my life away. I must tell him that.

Weiring I'm not saying that.

Katharina Thrown away.

Weiring I'm saying –

Katharina What *are* you saying?

Weiring Your youth. When you were young.

Katharina What about it?

Weiring When you were young.

Katharina My youth . . . (*She breaks off.*)

Weiring The things you did. The memories you have.

Katharina I don't remember much about it, to be honest.

Weiring You must. You must have memories.

Katharina Not really, no.

Weiring None?

Katharina Nothing comes to mind.

Weiring Try.

Katharina No.

Weiring But they're one of the best things about life. They –

Katharina Some people may think that.

Weiring Come on, of course you have mem—

Katharina All they bring is regrets. Those kind of memories. The memories you're talking about.

Weiring Better to have regrets than nothing at all.

Katharina So I have nothing?

Weiring All I want is . . . I don't want Christine's whole life happening in, in front of her, and her, and her just . . . staring at it. Thinking that's all she can do. (*He points.*) Sitting here – every day the same.

Katharina Christine didn't sit there . . . That's where your sister sat.

He looks at the chair.

Weiring I meant . . . (*He breaks off.*)

Katharina May she rest in peace . . . You were the best brother she could have had. She said that to me.

Weiring Did she? When?

Katharina A few times. (*Trying to lighten.*) I can't remember the exact dates . . . Your parents would have been proud of how you looked after her.

Weiring I did a good job of it.

Katharina Of course you did. Everyone round here says that.

Weiring She was young and so pretty –

Katharina And shy. Polite.

Weiring – and I thought I was being so clever and wise and . . . and *careful* . . . And one day I turned around and I looked at her and I didn't recognise her. She had grey hair. And wrinkles around her eyes . . . My little sister . . . My little sister, an old maid.

Katharina No. Not at all. She –

Weiring I *took* her life. I *deprived* her of it. To distinguish my own.

Katharina Herr Weiring . . .

Weiring Show how responsible I was. Important.

Katharina I have to . . . My husband . . .

Weiring I took it. I took her life. (*Looks at her chair.*) She used to look up at me. Smile.

Katharina She was perfectly happy, content . . .

Weiring As if she'd never expected anything more . . . As if I'd given her all she ever wanted . . . (*He indicates the chair.*) I can't look at it. I can't bear to look at it.

Mizi.

Mizi Hello?

Weiring Who is it?

Katharina Marie.

Mizi It's Mizi. It's so dark on the stairs I couldn't see where I was going.

Weiring The lamps should be lit by now.

Katharina Christine isn't here.

Mizi Oh.

Weiring She's gone out.

Katharina She was meeting you, wasn't she?

Mizi No . . . Yes . . .! She was. We must have missed each other. Oh well . . . Your husband told me you're off to a concert in the park.

Katharina Yes, we are. When did you speak to him?

Mizi Just now. He seems very keen . . . about going.

Katharina He loves his music. New hat?

Mizi Are you joking? It's last season's. I put new trimming on it.

Katharina You did that yourself?

Mizi Simple enough job.

Weiring She's very talented.

Katharina I keep forgetting she worked in a milliner's shop. But you left, didn't you?

Mizi Yes, I did.

Katharina But your mother tells me she wants you to go back.

Mizi She does.

Katharina Mothers are always right . . . How's her rheumatism? Or was it toothache?

Mizi They're gone. She just has this pain now, this nagging pain – she can't get rid of it. It just appears from nowhere and won't leave.

54

Weiring I should really be going. I'm going to be late. What time is it?

Katharina I'll walk down with you.

Weiring I had a coat.

Mizi Here.

Weiring But I was too warm with it.

Katharina Take it. It's supposed to get colder later.

Weiring Will I?

Pause. Christine.

Mizi Christine . . .

Katharina Back already?

Weiring What's wrong, darling?

Christine I have a splitting headache.

Weiring What's brought that on?

Katharina Perhaps the weather?

Weiring Light the lamp, Mizi.

Christine I can do it.

Weiring Let me take a look.

Christine Father, there's nothing to look *at*. It's inside my head.

Katharina Some people just can't take warm spring weather. The pressure.

Weiring Do you want me to stay here with you?

Christine No, don't be silly. You can't miss the show.

Weiring (*to Mizi*) Will you?

Mizi Course I will.

Christine It's really nothing.

Mizi When I have headaches I just want to be left alone.

Weiring Maybe you're tired?

Christine I'm fine. I am. (*Smiling.*) It's gone.

Weiring I love to see that smile. I'll see you later on.

He kisses her.

Katharina So what happened? . . .

Christine doesn't reply. Katharina indicates Weiring.

Tell him now. He has a right to know.

Weiring looks at Christine. Katharina moves away, takes Mizi with her.

Weiring What is it?

Christine (*after a pause*) I want you to hear what I've been doing. My singing. I've made progress.

Weiring I haven't time right now, Christine. I'll be late . . . I had my coat.

Katharina Here.

Weiring (*to Christine*) You'll be here when I get back?

Christine Yes.

Weiring You know how important you are to me, my darling.

He kisses her.
  He goes. Katharina too. Mizi looks at her.

Mizi We can relax now . . . What was that about?

Christine Nothing.

Mizi I know what it was about. (*Pause.*) The wine.

Christine What?

Mizi Last night. The wine they were pouring down our throats. That's what's caused your headache. Why don't I feel anything? I had more than you . . . Fun, wasn't it? They're something, the two of them. Think the world belongs to them. It does, in a way . . . And his apartment . . . Dori's place is the same. Your head still hurt? You're not saying much.

Christine He wasn't there.

Mizi Fritz?

Christine Of course Fritz!

Mizi He stood you up? Serves you right.

Christine How does it serve me right?

Mizi You do anything he wants. 'Yes, Fritz, of course, Fritz.' You spoil him. And spoilt men get arrogant.

Christine You talk such nonsense sometimes.

Mizi He's late every time he arranges to meet you. He doesn't bother to walk you home. He sits in an opera box cosying up to some woman . . . And now he hasn't turned up – no letter, no apology. And you accept it all without a murmur. Gaze at him with your big saucer eyes.

Christine I've seen you look at Theo.

Mizi I like looking at him. I like Dori, but he's not going to make me feel miserable and rejected.

Christine I'm not.

Mizi No man does that to me. The whole pack of them aren't worth it. They're not.

Christine I've never heard you talk like this before.

Mizi And d'you know why? Because we've never talked about these things before . . . I know how you feel about Fritz. I knew the moment you fell in love you'd be swept off your feet. It's how you are. You should be thankful I'm here.

Christine Should I?

Mizi To pour cold water on all the wild, romantic notions you've got in your head. Listen to me: you will feel like this about other men. You will fall in love . . .

Christine I don't want to. I don't care about other men. I'm not interested in other men.

Mizi That's exactly what they want to hear. 'All I want is you.' 'You're the only one.' As they go off in search of the next woman.

Christine Fritz isn't like that . . . (*Pause.*) The way he . . . How he touched me. He held me.

Pause.

Mizi It wears off.

Christine I don't want to listen to you.

Mizi I don't want you hurt.

Christine Will you go? Leave me alone.

Mizi I didn't mean to upset you.

Christine You have.

Mizi That's because you're easily upset. You have to be stronger.

Christine Get out! Get out of here. I don't want you in here.

Fritz.

Fritz Hello? Good evening.

Christine Fritz.

She runs to him, into his arms.

Mizi I won't stay.

She goes.

Fritz Let me breathe . . .

Christine She said you'll leave me.

Fritz I've come to see you.

Christine Don't. Don't leave me. Not yet.

Fritz Don't listen to her . . . What kind of a welcome's this?

Christine It's so good to see you.

Fritz (*strokes her*) Your lovely face.

Christine Where were you? Why didn't you come?

Fritz I was held up. I got there late. You'd gone. I started walking home but then . . . I wanted to see you. I wanted to see this face. Then I thought, why not just go there? So I walked over here and stood outside and . . . well, a few people looked at me, wondering what I was doing here, looking up at the windows. I had to ask a woman which flat you lived in.

Christine I don't care what people think.

Fritz Your father?

Christine Out.

Fritz So this is it? This is where Christine reigns supreme?

Christine It's dark, you can't see a thing.

She's about to take the shade off the lamp.

Fritz No, don't. I like it better like this . . . Is this where you work? This window? Is this where you sit? What a view. Right across the rooftops. What's that – the dark shape? There.

Christine The Kahlenberg.

Fritz The Vienna Woods, so it is. This is much better than my place.

Christine Don't be silly.

Fritz I'd love to live as high up as this. Look out across that. It's so quiet down there on the street.

Christine You wouldn't say that if it was the daytime.

Fritz What – coaches?

Christine Not round here. A locksmith has his workshop in the house opposite.

Fritz (*he touches her*) What sound does he make?

Christine Loud. I'm used to it now. I don't hear it any more.

Fritz It's exactly like I thought it would be.

He looks around the room more closely

Christine No, don't . . .

Fritz What are these pictures?

Christine Stop it. Don't look at them.

Fritz What's this one called?

Christine 'Parting'.

Fritz 'Parting' . . .? Very affecting.

Christine Shut up.

Fritz It is . . .! I like it.

Christine No you don't. I don't like it.

Fritz This one?

Christine 'Homecoming'.

Fritz 'Parting' and 'Homecoming'.

Christine They're awful. There's one in my father's room that's much better.

Fritz What's this one? What's she doing?

Christine It's a girl looking out of a window at the snow. It's called –

Fritz 'I Wish I Could Ski'.

Christine – 'Forsaken'.

Fritz (*puts lamp down*) And your books . . .

A small bookcase.

Christine Don't look at them, please . . .

Fritz Ah. Schiller. Hauff. An encyclopedia.

Christine Only the first volume.

Fritz Who's that humourless-looking bloke up there?

Christine Schubert.

Fritz Is it?

Christine Father loves his music. He used to compose songs too once, lovely songs.

Fritz Schubert or your father?

She smiles.

He doesn't now?

Christine Not any more.

A pause.

Fritz I could sit here for hours. What's this for?

Picks up a vase of artificial flowers.

Christine Are you going to ask about everything?

Fritz They're dusty.

Christine They are *not* dusty.

Fritz You should have real flowers in here. This room needs the smell of fresh flowers. The next time I come, I'll bring you . . .

He breaks off, turning away to hide his emotion.

Christine What is it?

Fritz Nothing. Nothing.

Christine What were you going to say?

Fritz I was going to say tomorrow I will send you fresh flowers.

Christine You won't give me a thought tomorrow.

He makes a defensive gesture.

Out of sight, out of mind.

Fritz No.

Christine Yes.

Fritz How can you say that?

Christine It's your fault. You never tell me anything about yourself. What you do all day.

Fritz What I do all day? You want to know? I'll tell you what I do, how mysterious it all is. I go to lectures – when the mood strikes me . . . Then on the way home, I drop in at a coffee-house. And while I'm there, I might read for a while . . . or I'll play the piano. Then I go and call on a friend and if they're not at home, I go and call on another one. So you see, I'm *vital* to the running of Vienna. So vital it bores me to talk about it . . . I should go.

Christine You just got here . . .

Fritz What about your father?

Christine He won't be back for ages yet. Stay a bit longer. Please.

Fritz But I have to . . . And Theo's waiting for me. I've things to talk over with him.

Christine Tonight?

Fritz Yes, tonight.

Christine But you'll be seeing him tomorrow . . .

Fritz I may not be in Vienna tomorrow.

Christine Why? Where are you going?

Fritz Something's come up. I'll only be gone for the day. Couple of days at most.

Christine Where?

Fritz Just somewhere. Don't look like that . . . I'm going to my parents' estate.

Christine You've never mentioned your parents before.

Fritz You want to hear about them? *I* don't. I only want to be with you. Alone with you.

Christine But I want more of you than just an hour grabbed in the evening. I see you, then you go again and we're no closer. Then the whole night drags by and every hour of the next day and I don't know where you are or who you're with, or what you feel.

Fritz Don't be sad.

Christine I long for you. It feels like you vanish and go somewhere far away . . .

Fritz Come on, that's –

Christine It's the truth. That's what I feel.

Fritz Come here. Right now – this moment – we're together; we're in love. Not for ever and ever. Here. Now. This is our eternity; the only one we have.

He kisses her.

I'm here with you and I don't want to be anywhere else or with anyone else, except you. All those rooftops out there, all the houses around us – we're hidden from them. We're so remote from the world . . . I feel so solitary, so alone with you. Safe from harm.

Christine When you say things like that, I can almost believe . . .

Fritz What, my darling?

Christine That you love me as much as . . . as I dream you do . . . Do you remember the first time you kissed me?

Fritz I do love you.

He embraces her, then breaks away.

You have to let me go . . .

Christine You regret saying it already?

Fritz No.

Christine You're free. You can go whenever you want. You've never promised anything – and I haven't asked you for anything. I don't care what happens to me – now that I've been happy once with you. I don't want anything more from life. But you have to know – I want you to know I've never been in love before – I've never loved anyone like this – and I won't love anyone again – if one day soon you decide you don't want me.

Fritz Don't say that. Don't . . . It sounds . . . too beautiful . . .

A knock on the door. Christine looks towards it, frowning.

It's Theo.

Christine He knows you're here?

Theodore.

Theodore Evening. Bit of a nerve, haven't I, gatecrashing like this.

Christine What's so important you had to come here?

Theodore I've been everywhere, looking for you.

Fritz (*undertone*) Why couldn't you wait downstairs?

Christine What are you saying to him?

Theodore He wants to know why I didn't wait downstairs. Which I would have done if I knew for certain you were here. But as I didn't much relish pacing back and forth for two hours . . .

Fritz You're still coming with me tomorrow?

Theodore Yes. I am.

Christine Where?

Fritz To my parents. Like I told you.

Theodore Can I sit down? I'm tired from chasing after him.

Christine Of course, please.

She busies herself near the window.

Fritz (*low*) Have you heard anything? How is she?

Theodore I don't know . . . What are you doing? You should be getting some sleep. Conserving your energy, not –

Christine rejoins them.

Fritz It's a wonderful view.

Theodore Rooftops. Very nice. (*To Christine.*) You don't get vertigo? It's a tad too high up for my taste.

Fritz That's what I like about it.

Theodore Right. We have to go. I have to take him from you, I'm afraid. We've an early start tomorrow.

Christine You really *are* going away?

Theodore He'll be back before you've even noticed he's gone.

Christine Will you write?

Theodore There'll be nothing *to* write. It's only one day. He'll be back the day after tomorrow.

Christine No, he'll be gone longer than that, I know he will.

Fritz winces.

Theodore Why do you say that? That's an idiotic thing to say.

Christine It's what I feel.

Theodore Do you always have to say everything you feel?

Christine Yes.

Theodore Idiotic . . .

Fritz Theo –

Theodore Honestly . . . You don't know anything.

Fritz Theo.

Christine What's he talking about?

Theodore I'm talking about how much of an idiot –

Fritz (*grabs him*) For God's sake –

Christine Get him out of here. Get him out.

Fritz We're going.

Theodore Kiss her goodbye, come on . . . Pretend I'm not here.

Christine I will.

Fritz and Christine kiss. Theodore puts a cigarette in his mouth, fumbles about for a match.

Theodore You wouldn't have a match . . . to light this damn thing?

Christine (*points to a box on the dresser*) Over there.

Theodore Empty.

She goes into the adjoining room.

Fritz I could be happy with her. Instead I'm lying through my teeth.

Theodore Don't be so dramatic. You'll laugh at yourself tomorrow.

Fritz I haven't much time left for that. At myself or anyone or anything.

Christine re-enters.

Christine Here.

Theodore Thank you. And goodbye. (*To Fritz.*) What is it now?

Fritz is looking around the room as though he wanted to take in everything again.

Fritz It's so hard to leave.

Christine Don't mock.

Fritz Why do you never believe me?

Theodore Fritz. We're going. Now. Say goodbye to her.

Fritz I'll see you again.

Christine Goodbye.

Theodore and Fritz exit. Christine stands looking depressed, then goes to the door which is standing open.

Fritz . . .

Fritz comes in again, takes hold of her. They embrace.

Fritz I have to go. I have to.

Act Three

Christine alone in the apartment.
  Weiring outside. Carrying lilac. Katharina.

Katharina I thought I heard someone.

Weiring Just me. The performance ran over tonight.

Katharina Did you manage to get tickets for us?

Weiring It went completely out of my head. I'll do it tomorrow.

Katharina What's that? In your hand. (*He shows her.*) More lilac?

Weiring You've caught me red-handed. To brighten up our apartment.

Katharina At this rate, there'll be no lilac left in the park.

Weiring She's upstairs, I should go up . . .

Katharina I haven't seen her for a few days.

Weiring She hasn't left the house.

Katharina Is she all right? What's the matter?

Weiring I tell her to go for a walk in the park – she doesn't want to. She's hardly said a word to me . . .

Katharina Did you know it's bad luck to bring lilac into a house?

Weiring Is it? I've never heard that. (*Offers a sprig.*) You won't want one then?

Katharina No, thank you. Goodnight.

He goes.

Christine by the window. Weiring. Christine turns to see who it is. Weiring sees her expectant face. He sits down. She goes to him, sits beside him, readies herself to speak. Lights down.

Lights. Christine at window again. Mizi.

Mizi What're you doing? You're just standing there.

Christine Are they back?

Mizi Are who back?

Christine Fritz –

Mizi How would I know? 'Hello, Mizi, how are you?'

Christine You haven't heard anything?

Mizi No.

Christine No letters for me?

Mizi No.

Christine Nothing from Theo?

Mizi sighs impatiently.

What?

Mizi No . . .! Nothing.

Christine Not a word for two days.

Mizi That's how long he said he'd be away.

Christine *One* day. Only one day. He's supposed to be back today.

Mizi They do what they want, you know that. They'll probably be gone a week. Have you been crying? Look at you. You should wash your face. What if your father sees you like this?

Christine He has seen me like this . . . I couldn't hide it. I told him.

Mizi Why?

Christine Finally. So he knows . . .! So he knows when Fritz comes here again. So he knows where I'm going in the evening.

Mizi What did he say?

Christine Nothing. He went out.

Mizi Went *out*?

Christine For a walk. He didn't object. He was –

Mizi Probably too stunned . . .

Christine No, he wasn't.

Mizi So he congratulated you? Is he going to give you away? Christine's going to be a June bride . . .

Christine turns her back on her.

You know what I think?

Christine Surprise me.

Mizi They made the whole trip up. They haven't gone away at all. They're right here in town. They're probably –

Christine They are not.

Mizi – strolling through the park right now.

Christine I went to his apartment last night.

Mizi You went all the way over there?

Christine The blinds were down. He's not home.

Mizi You're right. They did go away – to wherever . . . But they won't be coming back. Not to us . . . I'm only preparing you for the worst.

Christine He's coming back to me. When he came here . . . When he was here, in this room . . . You don't know him. He pretends to be like Theo – to not care, to be . . . flippant – but he's not. He was right here, beside me. He loves me. Maybe not for ever but for now. He'll come back to me.

Mizi I don't know Fritz at all.

Christine He'll come back – Theo too. Will you do something for me?

Mizi What?

Christine Go to Fritz's place . . .

Mizi No . . .

Christine Please . . .

Mizi I am not walking all the way over there . . . !

Christine Theo's, then . . . See if they're there. They will be. Having a drink. Please . . .

Mizi Why don't you go?

Christine He'll think I'm checking on him.

Mizi Well, you are.

Christine But he's not there . . . and Theo might have come back and know where he is . . . Please, Mizi, go for me.

Mizi You are so childish sometimes.

Christine It won't take you long. Please. Mizi.

Mizi I'm not going in – I'll just ask his servant.

Christine (*embraces her*) Thank you.

Mizi Anything to stop your whining.

Christine And come straight back.

Mizi My mother's expecting me. When I'm late I'll tell her it was your fault.

Christine I take full responsibility.

Mizi The things I do for you.

Christine I know.

Mizi If they're drinking, who knows, I might just stay . . .

She goes.
Christine tidies up the room, puts away her sewing things. She goes to the window, looks out.
Weiring and Katharina outside.

Katharina Herr Weiring, the tickets . . .

Weiring Did you hear?

Katharina Hear what?

Weiring She doesn't know.

Katharina Know what?

Weiring She doesn't know yet. I have to tell her.

Katharina What, Herr Weiring . . . ?

Weiring I have to go. I need to tell her. She doesn't know. I'll have to tell her.

Christine. Weiring. He watches her.

Christine Father . . .

Weiring Listen to me. I listened to you.

Christine If you don't like it, you'll have to throw me out because I won't –

Weiring Will you listen to me? . . . You're so young.

Christine I'm not. You might think that but I'm not.

Weiring This could just be –

Christine What?

Weiring I haven't been strict with you.

Christine No.

Weiring I could have said no. You're friends with Mizi. I let you go out. I pay for everything you need.

Christine I know that.

Weiring Have I not given you enough?

Christine I'll go if you want me to.

Weiring I'm not saying that! But if this is just some crush, which it could well be –

Christine It's not –

Weiring Next week, he's forgotten. You're thinking about something else . . . A month ago you wanted to be on the stage – nothing else mattered; it was life or death . . . I don't want you to be disappointed. You have so much life ahead of you . . . Look at me, old, creaky – but every day's a new day. And you're always part of it . . . Summer's almost here. You love summer; you always have. We'll start your singing again, we'll work at it, practise every day . . . I'll drive you out to the countryside in the holidays. There's so much to do. Do you want to give all that up – for something that may not be . . . Throw away your happiness on . . . It's not even real happiness.

Christine It is.

Weiring No. I'd know if it was. I'd have seen it in you. I haven't. Not true happiness.

Christine I'm happier with him –

Weiring Not this man –

Christine What do you know about him? Nothing.

Weiring You've told me.

Christine I wish I hadn't.

Weiring He won't understand. He won't appreciate you. Does he know how lucky he is? Does he understand how you feel?

Christine More than you do.

Weiring It's not love.

Christine It is. I love him.

Weiring It's simple-minded, it's . . . You haven't thought this through . . .

Christine You don't *think* love.

Weiring I want you to forget him.

Christine You haven't even met him.

Weiring You'll be as happy – more happy – with someone else. You might not think that now – but I'm telling you, you will. Someone who appreciates you.

Christine goes to the dresser to get her hat.

What are you doing?

Christine Going to him.

He restrains her.

Let go. Let me go.

He releases her.

Weiring Don't go now. I'll go with you tomorrow.

Christine You'll come with me? To his house?

Weiring We'll walk over there. You can't go out looking like that.

Christine To his house?

Weiring Yes. Now, sit down. You know I love you. You're my only child. Stay here with me for now. Will you?

Christine Yes, Father. (*She sits.*)

Weiring Good.

Mizi.

Christine Mizi . . .

Weiring What do you want?

Theodore, wearing black funeral clothes.

Mizi I met him on the street.

Christine Where's Fritz? Where is he? Tell me. Say something.

Theodore tries to say something. She looks around at them all, the truth dawning on her. She screams.

Weiring Christine . . . my darling . . .

Theodore You know all you need to.

Christine How? How did it happen? (*To Weiring.*) You knew? (*To Mizi.*) Did you know?

Mizi Theodore told me just now.

Theodore He fell. Fighting a duel.

Christine (*cries out*) Ah.

She almost collapses. Weiring holds her up.

Weiring Get out. Leave us.

Christine Why? Who killed him? . . . You must know who killed him.

Theodore It was no one you know.

Mizi Christine . . .

Christine Tell me! Someone tell me!

None of them speak. Again, she tries to leave. Her father holds her back.

I have a right to know why he was killed . . .!

Theodore It's not important.

Christine He died for nothing important? Tell me!

Mizi Christine, please stop . . .

Christine Another woman?

Theodore No.

Christine The black velvet dress. It was her.

She turns to Mizi.

He shot him. Didn't he? Her husband. And I . . . What am I? What was I to him? Did he give you anything for me? A note? . . . He didn't say anything? You didn't find . . . a letter? A note?

Theodore shakes his head.

He knew, didn't he? You both did. He already knew he might never come back . . . He kissed me and he walked out of that door to get himself killed for . . . for the black velvet dress . . . Didn't he know how much he meant –

Theodore He talked about you – as we . . . as we drove out yesterday.

Christine He talked *about* me . . .? What else did he talk *about*? How many other people, how many other things . . . He talked about me too. Oh God . . . What else? About his father and his mother and his friends and his room and springtime in the city and everything else in his life which he was leaving behind along with me. He talked to you about all of that as he drove out to get killed. But I should be grateful because he talked about me too . . .

77

Theodore He was . . . He had a lot of time for you.

Christine I was a pastime. But for her he was ready to die. I adored him. Didn't he know that? I gave him everything. I would have died for him. He left here smiling. Left this room and got himself shot for her.

Weiring Christine . . .

Christine What? What can you say to me?

Theodore (*to Mizi*) You really could have spared me this.

   She gives him an angry look.

I've had enough to do . . .

Christine I want to see him.

Theodore I don't think –

Christine I want to see him. One last time. Take me.

Theodore No, I can't . . . I –

Christine You can't refuse me . . . I want to. His face. A last time.

Theodore It's too late.

Christine How can it be too late?

Theodore He was buried this morning . . . It was a small funeral. Just close relatives and friends. The last couple of days have been . . . I had to tell his parents. And arrange the funeral, the guests . . .

Christine What am I then? Hm? What?

Mizi You didn't invite her to the funeral?

Theodore They would have wanted to know who she was. I wasn't in the mood for explaining – I was mourning.

Christine Less than all of them. Less than his relatives. Less than you.

Weiring My child, come here.

Theodore I don't have to explain – he was my best friend.

Weiring Please will you go?

Theodore I'm . . . I had no idea.

Christine What he meant to me? . . . Will you take me to his grave?

Weiring No –

Mizi Don't, Christine . . .

Theodore No.

Christine Leave me alone.

Weiring Christine, stay –

Mizi That woman might be there. Praying.

Christine (*stares ahead*) I'm not going to pray. No.

She rushes out.

Weiring Go after her. Quick.

Theodore and Mizi go after her. He walks to the window.

Christine, come back. Please come back.

End.